Contents

Close your eyes and sniff the air.
What can you smell?

Smell

Written by Mandy Suhr

Illustrated by Mike Gordon

The Senses

Hearing
Sight
Smell
Taste
Touch

First published in 1993 by Wayland Publishers
This edition printed in 2001 by Hodder Wayland,
an imprint of Hodder Children's Books

This revised edition published in 2007 by Wayland,
an imprint of Hachette Children's Books

Hachette Children's Books
338 Euston Road London, NW1 3BH

Reprinted in 2003

Series Editor: Mandy Suhr
Book Editor: Francesca Motisi
Editorial Assistant: Zoe Hargreaves
Consultants: Jane Battell
Cover Designer: Elaine Wilkinson

British Library Cataloguing in Publication Data
Suhr , Mandy
 Smell - (Senses series)
 I. Title II. Gordon, Mike III. Series
 612.8

Paperback ISBN 978-0-7502-5277-5

Printed in China

There are thousands of different kinds of smells.

Some smells are sweet...

some smells are stale.

Some things are nice to smell...

but some are not so nice!

Some smells can make
you feel hungry.

But sometimes, being able to smell
is not such a good thing!

Smells are made of tiny particles.
They float in the air and are so minute
that you can't see them.

When you breathe, these tiny
particles go into your nose.

They cling to the sticky mucus
that is inside your nose.

smell detectors

Under the mucus are special smell detectors. They collect the particles.

15

The particles stick to the smell detectors and they send messages to your brain. These messages help your brain to work out what kind of smell you are smelling.

All your senses work together but smell and taste are special partners.

When you smell something it helps you to work out what the taste will be like.

When you have a cold you can't smell so well.

This is because your nose is blocked. Often you cannot tell what things taste like either.

Some animals are really good at being able to smell. Dogs can find things just by smelling the scent that is left behind where something or someone has been. This is why dogs are often used to help find missing people.

Being able to smell things can sometimes warn you of danger.

Often you can smell things you might not be able to see, like gas, or something burning.

What is your favourite smell?

Play this game at school, or at home with a friend. Can you guess what these things are just by smelling them?

29

Notes for adults

'The Senses' is a series of first information books specially designed for the early stages of reading. Each book has a simple, factual text and amusing illustrations, combining reading for pleasure with fact-finding.

The content of the book addresses the requirements of the National Curriculum for Science, Key Stage One. The series takes a closer look at the human body, explaining very simply how we use each of our senses to learn about the world around us. This book explores the sense of smell.

The books are equally suitable for use at home or at school. Here are some suggestions for extension activities to complement the learning in this book.

1. Design a smell game using the one in this book as an example. This activity promotes collaborative

learning when carried out in small groups. It encourages discussion and hypothesizing, both important language skills.

2. Practise grouping and ordering skills. Smells can be grouped into sets and then ordered within their group. This involves designing experiments, discussion, using mathematical sets and provides a variety of opportunities for recording of results, eg graphs, tables. It also involves setting up and using data bases.

3. Make a class book about favourite smells or smells that children dislike.

4. Talk about situations where you might smell something that warns you of danger eg smoke/burning. Discuss the appropriate action to take in event of fire or other hazards.

Books to read

Body Books: Super Senses by Anita Ganeri (Evans Brothers, 2003)

How Do Your Senses Work? by A. Smith (Usborne Publishing Ltd, 2000)

Senses-abilities: Fun Ways to Explore the Senses by Michelle O'Brien-Palmer (A Cappella Publishing, 1998)

Senses: Smelling by Hartley, et al. (Heinemann, 2001)

Snapshot: Super Senses (Dorling Kindersley, 1996)